NOV 2 9 2016

W9-AVO-143

AFRICAN AMERICANS IN THE CIVIL WAR

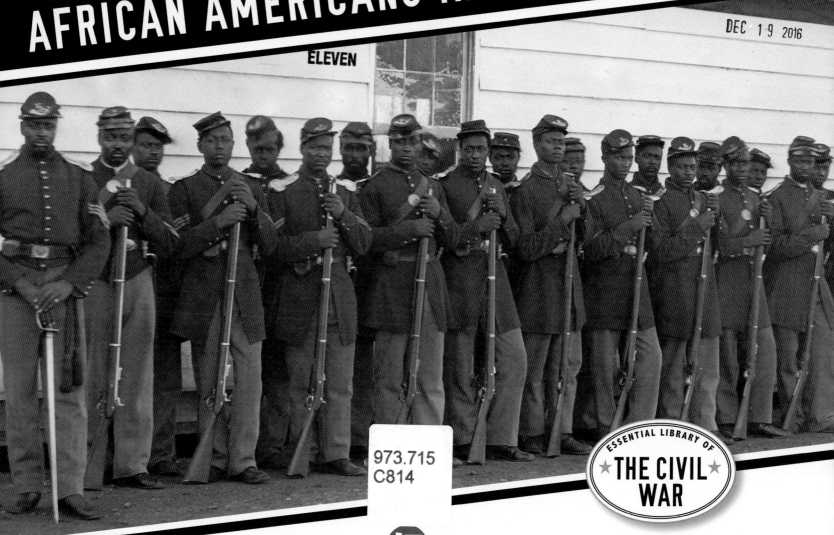

ELEVEN

Essential Library

An Imprint of Abdo Publishing
abdopublishing.com

ESSENTIAL LIBRARY OF
★ THE CIVIL ★
WAR

BY KARI A. CORNELL

CONTENT CONSULTANT

EDYTHE ANN QUINN, PHD
PROFESSOR OF HISTORY
HARTWICK COLLEGE

abdopublishing.com

Published by Abdo Publishing, a division of ABDO, PO Box 398166, Minneapolis, Minnesota 55439. Copyright © 2017 by Abdo Consulting Group, Inc. International copyrights reserved in all countries. No part of this book may be reproduced in any form without written permission from the publisher. Essential Library™ is a trademark and logo of Abdo Publishing.

Printed in the United States of America, North Mankato, Minnesota

032016
092016

Cover Photo: William Morris Smith/Library of Congress
Interior Photos: William Morris Smith/Library of Congress, 1; World History Archive/Newscom, 4, 39; Buyenlarge/Getty Images, 7; Schomburg Center for Research in Black Culture/Photographs and Prints Division/The New York Public Library, 9, 59; US National Archives and Records Administration, 10; John Reekie/Library of Congress, 13; AS400 DB/Corbis, 14, 53, 98 (top); Osborn & Durbec/Library of Congress, 19; Everett Collection/Newscom, 21; G. H. Houghton/Library of Congress, 22; Corbis, 26, 30, 44, 77; Everett Historical/Shutterstock Images, 28, 33, 50, 69, 91; Interim Archives/Getty Images, 35; Medford Historical Society Collection/Corbis, 40; The New York Historical Society/Getty Images, 47, 99 (top); Design Pics/Tom Patrick/Newscom, 55; Library of Congress, 60, 65, 71, 94, 96, 99 (bottom); Everett Collection Inc/Alamy Stock Photo, 63; The Miriam and Ira D. Wallach Division of Art/Prints and Photographs: Photography Collection/The New York Public Library, 67; Kean Collection/Getty Images, 72; Mathew Brady Picture History/Newscom, 75; The Protected Art Archive/Alamy, 79; S. B. Brown/Library of Congress, 83; L. Prang & Co./Library of Congress, 84; National Geographic Creative/Corbis, 87, 98 (bottom)

Editor: Jon Westmark
Series Designers: Kelsey Oseid and Maggie Villaume

Cataloging-in-Publication Data

Names: Cornell, Kari A., author.
Title: African Americans in the Civil War / by Kari A. Cornell.
Description: Minneapolis, MN : Abdo Publishing, [2017] | Series: Essential library of the Civil War | Includes bibliographical references and index.
Identifiers: LCCN 2015960295 | ISBN 9781680782714 (lib. bdg.) |
    ISBN 9781680774603 (ebook)
Subjects: LCSH: United States--History--Civil War, 1861-1865--Participation,
    African American--Juvenile literature. | African American soldiers--History--
    19th century--Juvenile literature. | United States. Army--African American
    troops--History--19th century--Juvenile literature.
Classification: DDC 973.7--dc23
LC record available at http://lccn.loc.gov/2015960295

CONTENTS

The Fifty-Fourth Massachusetts was the first official African-American Union regiment to fight in the Civil War.

THE BATTLE FOR FREEDOM BEGINS

As mortars exploded overhead, the soldiers of the Fifty-Fourth Massachusetts Infantry Regiment lined up on the beach in the faint light of the setting sun. Smoke filled the air, and the ground shook forcefully beneath their feet with each blast. It was July 18, 1863, more than two years into the American Civil War (1861–1865), and the Fifty-Fourth Massachusetts, the first all-black unit to be formed in the North, was about to get its first taste of military action. These men were tired and hungry after marching for two days with little food. But their commander, Colonel Robert Gould Shaw, could not turn down the offer to lead the charge on Fort Wagner, a Confederate stronghold near Charleston, South Carolina.

After all, the regiment was eager to fight, and Shaw had been requesting frontline assignments for months. Before starting down the beach, Shaw turned to his men and said, "I want you to prove yourselves. The eyes of thousands will look on what you do tonight."[1]

With his sword held high, Shaw led the charge, and the Fifty-Fourth began to advance down the narrow beach, hiding behind sand dunes along the way to avoid enemy fire. By the time the Fifty-Fourth was within firing range of the fort, Confederate soldiers had manned guns atop the ramparts and begun firing in what appeared to one soldier as "a sheet of flame."[2] The constant spray of bullets from Fort Wagner and five other Confederate forts nearby devastated the ranks of the Fifty-Fourth, taking out nearly half of the regiment's 624 men engaged in the assault.[3] Lewis Douglass, son of abolitionist leader Frederick Douglass and a soldier in the Fifty-Fourth, recalled the battle: "Not a man flinched, though it was a trying time. Men fell all around me. A shell would explode and clear a space of twenty feet [6 m]. Our men would close up again, but it was no use, we had to retreat. . . . I wish we had a hundred thousand colored troops. We would put an end to this war."[4]

With a handful of men, Shaw managed to reach the fort, scaling the sharp wooden stakes and wading through the waist-deep water that surrounded it. As Shaw climbed to the rampart he shouted, "Forward, Fifty-Fourth!"[5] Moments

Overtaking Fort Wagner and Morris Island would have been an important step in the Union's attempt to take Charleston, South Carolina.

later, Shaw was hit three times by gunfire. One of the bullets struck him in the chest, and he fell, dying along with some of his soldiers within the fort's walls.

TURNING POINT

Although the battle at Fort Wagner was a tragic loss for the Union, it was a turning point for African Americans throughout the nation. Before Fort Wagner, many whites doubted the bravery of black soldiers in Union blue, thinking they would cower and run when confronted by Confederate troops. But the African-American soldiers proved their critics wrong at Fort Wagner. In fact, it was here that the first US Congressional Medal of Honor was awarded to an African-American soldier, Sergeant William Carney. President Abraham Lincoln himself was deeply affected by the courage of the men of the Fifty-Fourth Massachusetts. Moving forward, Lincoln encouraged his Union generals to recruit African-American soldiers.

While General Ulysses S. Grant supported the arming of African-American soldiers, some Union generals resisted the idea of having black soldiers in their ranks. For them, President Lincoln had these terse words:

> You say you will not fight to free Negroes. Some of them seem to be willing to fight for you. When victory is won, there will be some black men who can remember that, with silent tongue and clenched teeth, and steady eye and well-poised bayonet, they have helped mankind on to this great consummation. I fear, however, that there will also be some white ones, unable to forget that with malignant heart and deceitful speech, they strove to hinder it.[6]

With the support of African-American communities and white allies in the North, African-American men appeared at local recruiting stations in droves, ready to sign up for military service with the Union. Approximately 180,000

WILLIAM H. CARNEY

1840–1908

Because of his heroism during the battle at Fort Wagner, Sergeant William Carney became the first black soldier to receive the Medal of Honor. Carney, who was originally from Norfolk, Virginia, was born into slavery. His father escaped to the North but had to leave his wife and son behind. His father bought Carney and his mother's freedom when Carney was a teenager. The family settled in New Bedford, Massachusetts, where Carney got an education and decided to join the ministry. But when Massachusetts governor John Andrew began to recruit men for an African-American regiment in early 1863, Carney changed his mind. He enlisted with the Fifty-Fourth Massachusetts Regiment in February 1863.

After five months of training, the Fifty-Fourth Massachusetts led the attack on Fort Wagner. During the charge to the fort, Carney was hit by a Confederate bullet, but it did not prevent him from taking action when he saw the regiment's flag bearer, Sergeant John Wall, go down. Carney quickly grabbed the flag and ran toward the front of his column. He was struck by multiple enemy shots but eventually arrived at the entrance to the fort. Alone, he then circled back, dodged fire, and joined the rest of his regiment. "Boys," Carney was said to announce, "The flag never touched the ground!"[7]

Carney was discharged from the military because of his injuries. He was later awarded the Medal of Honor for his bravery. When he died in 1908, the flag at the Massachusetts statehouse flew at half-mast in his honor.

African-American soldiers fought for the Union by the end of the war, including 33,000 free black men from the North.[8] Approximately 36,000 African Americans gave up their lives fighting for the Union.[9] The influx of black soldiers into the Union ranks beginning in early 1863 contributed greatly to the Union's eventual victory in the Civil War.

SOMETHING TO FIGHT FOR

Some may wonder why African Americans wanted to fight a war in a country where their people had been enslaved and treated so poorly for more than a century. The answer is freedom. In a war that ultimately decided the fate of slavery in the United States, African-American soldiers fought with dedication and conviction. Escaped slaves joined the Union army to fight for their freedom, while free African Americans signed up for Union regiments to destroy slavery and to fight for equal rights for themselves and for their people.

NOT YET CITIZENS

While free blacks in the North and South were no longer subject to slavery, they were not given equal rights of citizenship, either. They faced many restrictions on their daily lives, including what jobs they could have and where they could live. All were faced with the possibility of being mistaken for slaves, captured by slave catchers, and sold at auction. In the South, free African Americans needed to carry proof of their free status at all times. In most states, free African Americans could not vote, run for public office, or testify against a white person in court. And, long before federal income taxes became universal, African Americans were required to pay a tax on all the money they made. Many free African Americans believed fighting for the Union was a way to prove to the government they deserved full citizenship.

It was African Americans who had the most to gain in the Civil War—and the most to lose. Thousands of those who did not take up arms found other ways to contribute to the war effort. Many free blacks in the North helped gather supplies and food for African-American troops and runaway slaves living near Union army encampments. Some free African Americans were active in the abolitionist movement before and during the war, speaking out and writing articles to pressure the federal government to free the slaves. Others were simply trying to survive. The story of the African-American experience during the Civil War has as many variations as the number of people who lived through it. Few if any of those experiences were easy.

AFRICAN-AMERICAN WOMEN IN UNIFORM

At least two African-American women are known to have disguised themselves as men and joined the Union army as soldiers. At a time when physical examinations were glossed over to recruit as many able-bodied soldiers as possible, it was not difficult for a woman to pass as a young man. Maria Lewis served with the Eighth New York Cavalry, passing as a white male soldier. A comrade wrote that Lewis "skirmished and fought like the rest."[10] Lizzie Hoffman, from Winchester, Virginia, served with the Forty-Fifth US Colored Infantry.

Some African Americans performed labor for the Union, often doing tasks others did not want to do.

Field slaves young and old were forced to work long hours of manual labor.

SLAVERY IN THE SOUTH

In the years leading up to the Civil War, African Americans faced discrimination each and every day of their lives. Slaves were granted the fewest rights. James Curry, who was born into slavery in Person County, North Carolina, wrote of the day-to-day life of his mother, who worked in their slaveholder's home. Although the life of a domestic slave was thought to be considerably easier than the life of a slave who worked in the fields, Curry's mother was the only domestic, making her daily work very difficult.

On a typical day, she awoke at dawn, grabbed a pail, and headed to the barn to milk 14 cows before breakfast. She then hurried back to the kitchen to make bread for breakfast for the slave owner and his family. Some of the milk would be churned into butter; Curry's mother set up the butter churn and had one of the children begin

DOMESTIC SLAVES VS. PLANTATION SLAVES

Domestic slaves usually had a higher standard of living than those who worked in the fields. They had better living quarters and ate better food. If their slaveholders traveled, domestic slaves were sometimes brought along to help with the owner's children. At the same time, however, a domestic slave's interactions with the plantation mistress made them especially vulnerable to the mistress's scrutiny and abuse. Female slaves who were young and attractive were more likely to experience the wrath of their mistress, particularly when the mistress suspected her husband of favoring the slave. Domestic slaves also missed out on parties and the social culture at the slave quarters after hours.

Sometimes domestic slaves came to believe they were better than slaves who worked in the fields. It was not unusual for those who worked in plantation homes to refuse to associate with slaves who labored all day in the fields. When it came time for the children of domestic slaves to marry, parents often arranged for them to marry the children of other domestic slaves. Marriage to field slaves was often forbidden.

churning while she finished making breakfast. After clearing and washing the breakfast dishes for the slave owner, she began to make a simple breakfast for the slaves, which consisted of warm cornbread and buttermilk. The slaves had their breakfast at noon.

During the day, while other slaves were out working in the fields, Curry's mother was responsible for watching not only her own seven children but also those of the field slaves—approximately 10 to 15 children in all. In any spare time, she made the beds in the slaveholder's house and swept every room clean.

On different days throughout the week, she also washed and ironed the laundry. By late afternoon, she began to make dinner for the slave owner's family, usually roasted meat, vegetables, and bread with butter. Once again, she would quickly clear and wash the dishes to begin preparing dinner for the slaves, who ate between 8:00 and 9:00 in the evening. The slaves' dinner was often cornbread or potatoes and any leftover meat from the slave owner's dinner. If no meat remained, each slave received one herring. Then, after clearing and washing dishes for the last time that day, she headed back to the barn to milk the cows again.

Only after these tasks were complete was Curry's mother allowed to leave her owner's house and return to her own simple log cabin. By then it was usually 9:00 or 10:00 at night, and she was exhausted from the day's work. But this was the only time she had to tend to her own family's needs. Often, the children's clothes needed mending. Slave owners

FROM MATERNAL CAREGIVER TO SLAVE

James Curry's mother was responsible for caring for the owner's children when they were young. But once the children grew older, the loving relationship changed to that of owner and slave. This shift was common among white children and their African-American caregivers throughout the South. Curry told the story of one of the owner's daughters, who was home from school and had a problem with the dinner Curry's mother served:

[S]he struck my mother, who pushed her away, and she fell on the floor. Her father was not at home. When he came, which was while the slaves were eating in the kitchen, she told him about it. He came down . . . with a hickory rod, he beat her fifteen or twenty strokes, and then called his daughter and told her to take her satisfaction of her, and she did beat her until she was satisfied.[1]

typically did not provide much in the way of clothing, so patches and stitches prolonged the life of the few clothes each child had. Curry's mother would mend through the night on a chair by the fire, taking short naps every so often. Just before dawn, she would crawl into bed for a couple of hours before getting up and beginning her chores for the next day.

FOOD, CLOTHING, AND SHELTER

Many people take the basic necessities of food, clothing, and shelter for granted. But as Curry's story indicates, slaves in the South had barely enough of what they needed to live.

Slaves typically ate a small breakfast and a late dinner in their own cabins. Lunch was prepared by an older slave who worked in the main kitchen of the home. The food was often the same each day, consisting of cornmeal, lard, peas, greens, molasses, flour, and whatever leftovers slave owners were willing to share. One slave remembered a typical lunch on the plantation: "The peas, the beans, the turnips, the potatoes, all seasoned up with meats and sometimes a ham bone, was cooked in a big iron kettle and when meal time come they all gathered around the pot for a-plenty of helpings!"[2]

The amount of food provided to slaves depended on the slave owners, but many fed them as little as possible to keep costs low. The food was not particularly nutritious, either. Many slave owners were not concerned with the

Plantation slaves often lived in outbuildings with few accommodations.

overall health of slaves, as they could replace them after six or seven years. Many slaves were often hungry, and it was common for them to steal food from the owner's kitchen. Those who did, however, faced severe punishment if caught.

Some slaves, particularly those in the southernmost slave states, were allowed to grow their own gardens on small plots of land. In some cases, they were also allowed to sell surplus food grown in their gardens to earn money. If slaves had time after the long workday, some went fishing or hunting to supplement the meals their owners provided. They hunted raccoons, squirrels, birds, and deer.

Clothing, too, was an added expense few owners wanted to spend on slaves. Slave owners usually distributed clothes once per year, often at Christmastime. Slaves' clothes were made of inexpensive fabrics designed to be durable rather than comfortable. Slaves sometimes received raw fabric and were expected to cut and sew their own clothes. House slaves tended to be clothed more formally— often with hand-me-downs from the owner's family. Children were typically given only a long shirt and little else until their teen years.

On plantations, slave homes were little more than flimsy shacks built of sticks with dirt floors and little if any furniture. In winter months, wind whipped through the cracks between the wallboards, giving slaves—many of whom slept on the dirt floors—almost no protection against the cold. Domestic slaves, on the other hand, sometimes slept in a room in the slave owner's house.

FAMILY TIES

For those slaves whose families had not been separated, family meant everything, especially since they knew that at any time, an owner could sell a husband, wife, brother, sister, mother, father, son, or daughter to another plantation or household, sometimes hundreds of miles away. The term *family* was also used to include family friends. Elder men or women who cared for children when the parents were working in the fields, for example, were considered family. Slaves who worked together at the same plantation but were not related by blood might consider themselves family as well. One of the greatest fears of slaves in upper slave states, such as Virginia, was

Some slave owners afforded field slaves so little clothing the slaves wore tattered rags.

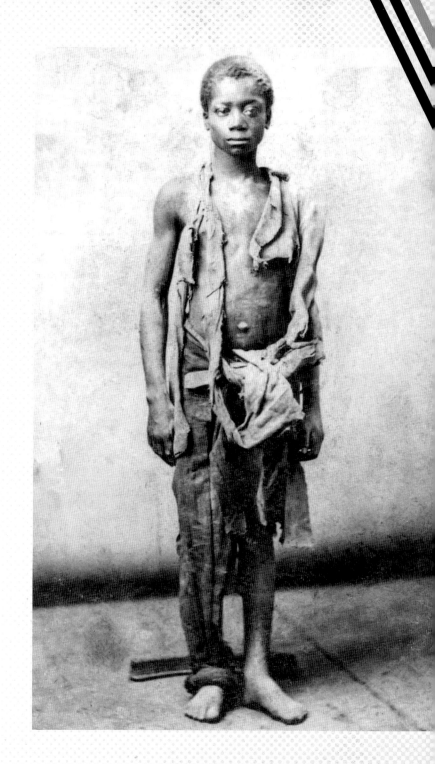

Because slaves were seen as property, slave owners often prioritized economic benefit over family continuity when considering whether to sell a slave.

that a family member would be sold farther south, where they would be nearly impossible to find.

As slavery expanded west into the new states of Missouri and Texas in the first half of the 1800s, slaves were constantly uprooted from familiar plantations in the Southeast, separated from families and friends, and taken to slave markets, where they were sold for profit. Most never saw family again, and some died on the difficult journey west.

Romantic relationships between male and female slaves were either strongly encouraged or discouraged, depending on the circumstances and the slaveholder. If the same person owned both slaves, relationships were beneficial to the owner, as he could sell any children the couple had for profit. In cases where different people owned the slaves, the owner of the female slave typically supported the union, as any children the female slave might have automatically became the property of the mother's owner. The owner of the male slave, on the other hand, did not benefit financially if the couple had children. He often did not support the union.

Many female slaves lived with the constant threat of rape or other sexual abuse. Instances of slave owners forcing female slaves to have sexual relations with them were rampant. The children born as a result of these owner-slave relationships sometimes received special treatment from the slave owner.

SLAVE CODES

All slaves were forced to follow certain rules in society. These rules were not always the same in each state, but a handful remained consistent throughout the slave states. Here are the common rules:

- It was illegal to do business with a slave without the owner's permission.
- Slaves could be given as gifts or raffle prizes.
- Slaves could not testify against a white person in a court of law.
- It was against the law for slaves to learn to read or write.
- In Missouri, anyone caught teaching slaves faced six months in prison and a fine of $500 or more.
- It was against the law for slaves to meet with one another without a white person present.
- Law did not recognize marriages between slaves.
- Slaves who were suspected of committing arson, raping a white person, or planning to rebel or escape were sentenced to death.

In other instances, they were sold to faraway plantations without a moment's hesitation.

Some slaveholders also forced their female slaves to have sexual relations with male slaves, with the goal of producing more slaves for the owner. This had a devastating effect on female slaves and their families, but they were powerless to stop it.

DIFFERENCES ACROSS THE SOUTH

Slaves across the South suffered abuses at the hands of their owners, though treatment did vary, especially between the Lower South and the Upper South. The Lower South included Alabama, Louisiana, Mississippi, South Carolina, Georgia, Florida, Arkansas, and Texas. Slaves living on plantations, which were more common in the Lower South, were forced to work long hours with few breaks to grow crops for their owners. Slave drivers sometimes whipped those who could not keep up with the hard labor.

Field labor was less common in the Upper South, which was composed of Virginia, Maryland, North Carolina, Delaware, Kentucky, Tennessee, and Washington, DC. In this part of the country, many tobacco plantations turned to vegetable and wheat farming in the early 1800s, eliminating the need for large numbers of slaves. Without plantations, many slave owners did not feel the need to work slaves for long hours, so the living conditions were more relaxed. It was not uncommon, for example, in the Upper South, especially in cities, for slave owners to rent out their slaves to shipyards, warehouses, brickyards, or cotton factories. Employers paid slaves' wages to their owners, but the slaves had more freedom to move around within the community. Some slaves were allowed to keep a small portion of their wages for themselves.

If a slave in the Upper South disobeyed, however, some slave owners punished them by selling them farther south. So although many slaves in the Upper South had a slightly easier life than slaves in the Lower South, the threat of being sold always loomed.

WARTIME CHANGES

When the Civil War broke out on April 12, 1861, life for slaves throughout the Confederate states began to change. Southern slave owners left their plantations

Confederate home guards worked to make sure slaves did not run away during the war. Slaves caught without passes were punished.

to fight for the Confederacy, in many cases leaving their wives to manage the day-to-day operations of their estates. Although most of these women were well versed in household management, many had little experience running a farm or plantation, let alone maintaining control over a large number of slaves.

As a result, slaves on plantations tended to have more freedom. They sometimes left their owner's farms during the day to visit friends or relatives at nearby plantations. They refused more of their owners' demands, ignored curfews, and took larger portions of food. Greater numbers of enslaved African Americans attempted to escape to the North while their male slave owners were off at war. But for slaves searching for freedom, the journey was perilous and the future uncertain.

FREE AFRICAN AMERICANS IN THE SOUTH

At the time of the Civil War, slavery had existed in the United States for more than 200 years. During that time, a significant number of African-American families had gained their freedom. Some had successfully run away from their owners, others had saved enough money over time to buy freedom, and still others were granted freedom by their slave owners. But by today's standard, free blacks who lived during the Civil War were anything but free. Every day they felt the effects of living in a country where their people were enslaved.

A family of former slaves outside their rundown home in Fredericksburg, Virginia.

Despite the commonly held notion that most free blacks lived in the North in the years leading up to and during the Civil War, just the opposite was true. Out of the 488,070 free blacks who lived in the United States in 1860, 261,918 lived in the South and 226,152 lived in the North.[1] Many African Americans chose to stay in the South after they became free because the South was their home, and they had families there. It was not uncommon for families to include members who were slaves and others who were free. The free often worked and saved to purchase freedom for their enslaved family members. In other cases, free blacks stayed in areas they had lived in all their lives because their former owners had granted them plots of land in their wills.

RESTRICTIONS IN THE SOUTH

Free African Americans living in the slave states at the time of the Civil War faced particular restrictions. If free blacks in the Upper South were convicted of crimes, even minor offenses, they could be sold

BREAKING THE LAW

In the 1800s, several Southern states passed laws declaring blacks were required to leave the state once they were set free. In Virginia, for example, African Americans set free after 1806 were expected to leave the state. Those who did not leave risked being enslaved. Virginia passed another law in 1831 that allowed local sheriffs to sell free black people in slave auctions. In North Carolina, it was against the law for free blacks to enter the state.

Free African Americans who wished to stay in Southern states could petition the government to allow them to remain. In other instances, free blacks simply ignored the laws and stayed put. Often, the whites who knew of free blacks living in states with these laws did not bother to report violations. Though the laws existed, they were not consistently enforced.

SLAVERY IN VIRGINIA

Virginia planters began purchasing slaves in the late 1600s and continued to buy them throughout the 1700s to tend their labor-intensive tobacco crops. But by the time of the Revolutionary War (1775–1783), overplanting had begun to deplete the soil, making it difficult to grow tobacco. Tobacco planters had also become tired of the rising and falling price of tobacco, so they began to transition to food crops. With this shift, farmers needed fewer slaves to tend fields. Plantation owners kept the slaves they needed and either set the others free, rented them to others, or sold them to cotton plantations in the Lower South. With a surplus of slaves, Richmond, Virginia, became home to the busiest slave market in the country. Virginia slaveholders bred and sold slaves for profit. But it was not only Southerners profiting from slavery. Northern banks offered loans to Southerners to purchase additional slaves. The banks collected interest in return.

into slavery farther south. In states such as Virginia, African Americans were required to leave the state once they were granted freedom, but many chose to stay put, taking the risk of being enslaved once more. Free blacks living in Washington, DC, had to abide by curfews and follow other rules that did not apply to whites.

In the Lower South, the vast majority of free African Americans lived in urban centers. Jobs were plentiful in these cities, but restrictions still persisted. In Charleston, South Carolina, free blacks were required to wear badges to work. These badges were used to ensure that African Americans of mixed descent could not pass as white. Higher-paying jobs, such as those in mechanical trades, were difficult for blacks to acquire because of white discrimination. The risk of being mistaken for an escaped slave or otherwise forced into slavery was also most acute in the Lower South. In 1859, for example, the South Carolina government formed the Committee on the Colored Population, with the sole intent of enslaving all free blacks living within the state slaves.

Free African Americans in the South typically held low-paying jobs as domestic servants, cooks, laundresses, porters, sailors, and shipyard workers. But there were also opportunities for work in better-paying jobs in skilled trades. In addition, some free African Americans started their own businesses as barbers, shopkeepers, and tailors.

The threat of being captured and sold into slavery was real for free African Americans in the South.

During the war, free blacks in the South were eligible for government aid from the Confederacy, but most did not receive it due in large part to prejudice. The little food or clothing that was available was diverted to white families affected by the war. As a result, shortage of goods and the general devastation of warfare affected free African Americans more profoundly than other groups within Southern communities. Like poor Southern whites, free blacks sometimes resorted to stealing and looting to acquire enough food to survive.

Because of the discrimination they faced, many free African Americans in the South supported the Union during the war, even if they did not voice these opinions publicly. William James, a free black man who lived in Henrico County, Virginia, explained why he supported the Union: "I believed that if the [Confederates] gained their independence they would make slaves of all of us free colored people."[2]

IN THE CONFEDERATE ARMY

In Confederate states, enslaved African Americans were forced to take part in the war effort. Many male slaves were taken from plantations and impressed into the Confederate army, where they cooked, did laundry, built fortifications, and dug trenches. Between 3,000 and 6,000 African Americans went into battle on the side of the Confederacy.[3] Northern abolitionist Frederick Douglass published accounts of blacks serving and even fighting for the Confederacy in his

A Union officer, *right*, detains a Confederate soldier, *left*, and his slave.

antislavery newspaper, *Douglass' Monthly*. He wanted to convince his Northern audience that having African-American troops was giving the South a distinct advantage and that the Union army should recruit willing African Americans.

One of Douglass's sources was William Henry Johnson, a free black man from Connecticut who fought with Union troops despite the federal government's ban. At the First Battle of Bull Run in July 1861, Johnson reported seeing three Confederate regiments, from Georgia, South Carolina, and Virginia. Of the battle, Johnson said, "It was not alone the white man's victory, for it was won by slaves. Yes, the Confederates had three regiments of blacks in the field, and they maneuvered like veterans, and beat the Union men back. This is not guessing, but it is a fact."[4]

If slaves willingly fought on the side of the Confederacy, it is likely they were promised freedom in exchange for their military service. John Parker, a slave from Virginia, is one example of an African American who was first impressed into the Confederate army and later forced to fight. At first, Parker was ordered to build batteries and fortifications in Richmond, Virginia, which he did. Afterward, he was sent with three other slaves to fight with the Confederate army in the First Battle of Bull Run. He was promised freedom and payment to fight.

Parker remembered hoping above all else that he would not be killed and that the North would win the battle. "We wished to our hearts that the Yankees would whip us. . . . We would have run over to the other side, but our officers would have shot us if we had made the attempt."[5]

RAISING THEIR OWN REGIMENTS

Some cities in the South were home to a free black aristocratic class. This group, which identified with the planter class—white families that owned plantations—existed in Charleston; New Orleans, Louisiana; and Natchez, Mississippi. Representing the wealthiest free blacks in the United States, approximately 3,700 African Americans in this class owned slaves.[6] Aristocratic blacks existed in a middle ground of social structure, above slaves, above working-class free blacks, but beneath whites. Aristocratic free blacks enjoyed a level of independence and freedom unknown to other free blacks in the North or South. In an effort to gain acceptance among elite whites and better treatment within society, free black aristocrats founded their own churches, schools, and charitable organizations.

When the war began, aristocratic free blacks in the South worked hard to show their devotion to the Confederate

ELITE BLACKS IN NEW ORLEANS

In the years leading up to the Civil War, free people of color in New Orleans experienced rare privileges in a community where they felt accepted. While African-American elite existed in other Southern and Northern cities, New Orleans was different. As a vibrant port city that had been a mix of French, Spanish, English, African, and Caribbean settlers for more than a century, the people of New Orleans were more accustomed to racial diversity. Blacks of the social elite in New Orleans were able to easily blend in as Creole, the name adopted by white descendants of early French and Spanish settlers. Within this unique culture, black elites were able to prosper in society and acquire status that was nearly equal to that of wealthy whites.

cause, going so far as to form their own military regiments. In New Orleans, African-American soldiers formed the First, Second, and Third Louisiana Native Guard. The First Kansas Colored Volunteer Infantry and the First South Carolina Infantry, African Descent, formed in the same way. A group of wealthy free blacks in Charleston expressed their allegiance to the Confederate elite in their community:

> *In our veins flows the blood of the white race, in some half, in others much more than half white blood. . . . Our attachments are with you, our hopes and safety and protection from you. . . . Our allegiance is due to South Carolina and in her defense, we will offer up our lives, and all that is dear to us.*[7]

Ironically, the free blacks who sought to gain acceptance by fighting for the Confederacy were denied the opportunity. The Confederacy did not allow the self-initiated regiments into battle. When Union troops took control of the cities where these regiments formed, many of the regiments switched sides and pledged their allegiance to the Union. By the time the Confederacy passed General Orders Number 14 on March 13, 1865, allowing black regiments to fight for the South, none of the self-formed black regiments joined to fight for the Confederacy.

Led by naval forces, the Union took New Orleans on May 1, 1862. Free African Americans in the city soon allied themselves with the Union cause.

Competition for skilled jobs was greater in the North than in the South.

FREE AFRICAN AMERICANS IN THE NORTH

In the late 1700s and early 1800s, states throughout the North, which had practiced slavery since colonial times, took action to get rid of slavery within their borders, freeing thousands of African Americans. Free blacks in the North lived primarily in large cities such as New York City; Boston, Massachusetts; Philadelphia, Pennsylvania; Cincinnati, Ohio; Detroit, Michigan; and Chicago, Illinois. In the 1840s and 1850s, many free blacks from the South made their way to the North, in many cases leaving behind friends and family members, in hopes of living in a place where they had more rights and opportunities. But many discovered life in the Northern states fell far short of their expectations.

Much to the surprise of free blacks who had worked for a time in the South, fewer jobs in skilled trades were available to them in the North. This was because far more immigrants settled in the North, creating greater competition for skilled-labor jobs than in the South. The jobs available to blacks in the North—domestic servants, cooks, laundresses, porters, sailors, and shipyard workers—offered wages that scraped the very bottom of the pay scale. This was due in large part to the existence of labor unions, organizations that represented workers in meetings with company managers. The unions were pressured by Northern whites and Western European immigrants—mainly Irish—to deny blacks skilled labor jobs or apprenticeships. Immigrants wanted these jobs for themselves because they offered higher pay, and Irish immigrants held more sway with labor unions because of their skin color.

For free blacks from the South who had experience working as blacksmiths, carpenters, or in other trade professions, this was a tremendous setback, as they

BLACK PREJUDICE

In addition to the prejudice expressed by Northern whites toward African Americans, some African Americans who had lived in the North for many years before the war looked down on free blacks who came from the South. They claimed the newcomers reinforced the misconception that blacks were uneducated, loud, and lacked manners, stereotypes black Northerners had worked hard to overcome.

were forced to take lower-paying jobs if they could find employment at all. In Philadelphia, employment records from the 1850s state that "the greater number [of black workers] are compelled to abandon their trades on account of the unrelenting prejudice against their color."[1]

BLACK CODES

In the North, free African Americans had to abide by laws called Black Codes, which restricted their freedom in many ways. In some areas of the North, including Ohio, Indiana, Michigan, and Illinois, free blacks were required to make payments to prove to whites that they were responsible members of society. Oftentimes, blacks in these states had to find a white person to vouch for their good character in order to get a job or rent a place to live.

Rules also dictated where blacks could live. In cities home to a large population of African Americans, such as Cincinnati, neighborhoods were sometimes segregated

LIVING CONDITIONS

Few Northern free African Americans lived in the same neighborhoods as whites. Instead, blacks in cities such as Boston, Cincinnati, New York, and Philadelphia lived together in neighborhoods separated by race. More often than not, blacks were forced to live in neighborhoods with unsanitary conditions that caused disease. In fact, a study conducted in 1846 concluded that almost every black baby born into poverty in Philadelphia that year died within months of birth.

Well-to-do African Americans lived in better conditions but were still denied access to homes within white neighborhoods, as whites feared the black residents would bring down property values. Vibrant black communities, such as the Beacon Hill neighborhood in Boston, where blacks lived in "modest and closely set buildings," emerged, providing free African Americans a place to call home.[2]

African-American children had greater opportunity to attend school in urban areas of the North compared to rural areas.

based on skin color. Those with the darkest skin color were forced to live in the most downtrodden areas, including Bucktown, a community known for its poverty and poor sanitary conditions.

Education available for free African-American children in the mid-1800s was often inferior to the education offered to white children in the same communities. Nearly all states in the North provided public schools for African Americans by 1860. However, many public school systems were segregated, and although whites and free African Americans both paid taxes to fund schools, African-American schools did not receive the same funding as white schools. As a result, schools for African-American children were often run-down, overcrowded, and in short supply of teachers.

Free African Americans in the North also experienced segregation every time they tried to go to the theater, eat in a restaurant, stay in a hotel, or ride a stagecoach. Often, African Americans were not permitted to use these services. Other times, they were made to use theaters, restaurants, or hotels designated for blacks only, which businesses often chose not to maintain as well as those reserved for white patrons.

But perhaps the most blatant form of discrimination free blacks in the North endured before the Civil War was open hostility from Northern whites. Although it was true that many more whites in the North disapproved of slavery than those in the South, many Northerners held a low opinion of African Americans. And unlike white Southerners, most whites in the North had little experience living in communities with African Americans. In the eyes of many whites, blacks were lazy, dependent, unintelligent, and untrustworthy. In the early years of the

Civil War, this sentiment became clear in white Northerners' unwillingness to allow African Americans to fight in the war. A columnist for the *New York Tribune* wrote, "Loyal Whites have generally become willing that [African Americans] should fight, but the great majority have no faith that they will really do so. Many hope they will prove cowards and sneaks—others greatly fear it."[3]

DRAFT RIOT OF 1863

On July 13, 1863, violent protests broke out in New York City. The protests were in response to a new draft law. The law made it mandatory for white men within a certain age range to enlist in the Union army, but a loophole allowed wealthy Northerners to buy their way out of military service. Because African Americans were not considered citizens, they too were exempt from the draft. Many of the protesters were working-class immigrants, particularly Irish, who could not afford to buy their way out of the military service. They were upset that the burden of serving in the Civil War fell on working-class whites. They were also worried African Americans from the South would soon flood into the city and take their jobs.

The African-American community suffered most during the protests. Rioters sought out and attacked African Americans. At least 11 black men were violently murdered. The houses of poor blacks were systematically burned, as was the Colored Orphan Asylum, which was home to 237 children, all of whom escaped safely. By the time 6,000 Union troops arrived to restore order on July 17, New York City was in shambles, with an estimated 119 people killed.[4] In the aftermath of the riots, 20 percent of the city's African-American population chose to leave.[5]

Northern racial prejudice toward African Americans escalated to violence in

AFRICAN-AMERICAN COMMUNITIES

One advantage free blacks in the North had over those in the South was the freedom to organize and meet with other free blacks. In Northern cities with large African-American communities, such as Boston, New York, and Philadelphia, free blacks were able to form their own civic groups. People met regularly at black churches, community meetings, and black Masonic lodges.

Through involvement with Masonic lodges, many leaders within African-American activist communities learned how to organize and how to

VIGILANCE COMMITTEES

Posters announcing, "The Slave-hunter is among us! Be on your Guard! An arrest is planned for To-Night" were posted in Northern cities, warning African Americans of potential danger.[6] Under the Fugitive Slave Act of 1850, which granted local governments the authority to capture and return runaway slaves to their owners, no African American was safe. Even free blacks living in Northern states worried about being captured by slave catchers and sold to plantations in the South. Until 1864, slave catchers could catch and sell blacks into slavery in the South without proving the captured man or woman was a slave in a court of law. This put many African Americans at risk. Leaders and abolitionists within free African-American communities in many cities advised blacks to carry a gun at all times to defend themselves against such attacks. Vigilance committees, organizations formed in the 1830s by abolitionist free blacks and whites, stepped forward to provide protection for African Americans. In the years after the Fugitive Slave Act was passed, these groups also arranged safe passage to Canada for fugitives.

navigate the federal political system. Black churches provided a place to worship and a sense of hope to African-American members. But more than that, black churches provided a sense of belonging and solidarity among fellow blacks within the community. As far back as the founding of the African Methodist Episcopal Church in Philadelphia in 1787, churches were gathering places in African-American neighborhoods. In Boston, for example, the African Baptist Church was also called the African Meeting House. In this way, churches became important venues for discussions about racial injustice.

General black community meetings also sprang up throughout the North as a way for free blacks to gather and air their grievances about racial prejudice. These meetings, which were announced in black newspapers, became a forum for debates and discussions about abolition, civil rights, and other issues that affected the black community. All of these meetings served a larger purpose: they provided the means for leaders within the black community to set an agenda and begin to organize. These leaders formed the backbone of the abolitionist movement and also rallied African Americans to take up arms to fight to destroy slavery.

Escaping slaves cross the Rappahannock River in Virginia in August 1962.
A nearby battle allowed fugitive slaves to escape unnoticed.

RUNAWAYS AND CONTRABAND

The thought of attempting to escape surely crossed the minds of many African Americans enslaved by the Confederacy at the start of the Civil War, but very few attempted to make it to freedom. The risks were simply too great, especially for those enslaved in the Lower South. Escaped slaves who made it into Union territory could be treated in a number of different ways. Sometimes the Union army viewed escaped slaves as captured enemy property, while other times the slaves were returned to their former owners. On August 6, 1861, President Lincoln signed an act of Congress into law that helped clarify the status of escaped slaves. The First Confiscation Act stated that slaves captured by the Union were no

UNDERGROUND RAILROAD

The Underground Railroad was a network of secret routes, called lines, and safe houses, called stations, across 14 states that provided escaped slaves with a path to freedom in the North. Fugitives using the Underground Railroad usually traveled 10 to 20 miles (16 to 32 km) between stops. Hidden in barns, attics, or crawl spaces to avoid detection, escaped slaves would rest and have food before moving on the next night.

Free blacks, former slaves, and white allies who helped fugitives along the way were called conductors. Harriet Tubman was one of the most well-known conductors. Tubman was an escaped slave living in Auburn, New York. In the 11 years preceding the Civil War, Tubman is believed to have made 19 trips south to help 70 slaves out of Maryland. She helped another 60 or so make their way from the North into Canada, where slavery was against the law.[1] Tubman made her last trip in November 1861.

longer the property of their slave owners and were instead under the control of the Union.

MAKING A BREAK FOR IT

As Union regiments made their way farther into Confederate territory, slaves in the Upper South—in states such as Tennessee, Virginia, and Kentucky—began to take their chances and head for Union lines. In these areas, where escape was only a few hours' walk away, slaves could almost taste freedom. Before the war began, it was generally only young, strong men who attempted escape. But with the safety of Union lines so near, women, children, and older slaves also attempted to escape. They dressed in dark clothing, stuffed provisions for the journey into their pockets, and crept off into the blackness of night. Escaping slaves walked as far as they could during the first leg of their journeys, trying to put as much

Abolitionist Harriet Tubman, *left*, stands with family and friends after escorting them to freedom.

distance between them and their former owners' homes as possible. When they needed rest, they often hunkered down in tall grasses or wooded areas and tried to sleep. The sound of barking dogs in the distance would be enough to startle them awake and keep them moving. Slave catchers used dogs to track the scents of escaping slaves.

For those escaping from Kentucky or Tennessee, crossing the Ohio River was their last obstacle to freedom. Many slaves made their way across the river and into Cincinnati, home to a large free black population and an active abolitionist movement. Abolitionists such as John Rankin, a white Presbyterian minister who lived with his wife, Jean, and their 13 children on a hill above the Ohio River, helped thousands of slaves escape between 1822 and 1865 by offering his home as a stop on the Underground Railroad.[2] Others also helped, including John P. Parker, a former slave who helped approximately 400 fugitive slaves to freedom by ferrying them across the Ohio River to safety in the North.[3]

After the First Confiscation Act, slaves who were taken up by the Union army were not free but were instead seen as contraband, or seized property, by the US government. President Lincoln was concerned that giving escaped slaves their freedom would convince border states such as Kentucky, Maryland, and Missouri, which allowed slavery, to join the Confederacy. However, with growing support in the Union for freeing slaves, Congress drafted the Second Confiscation Act, which would free all former slaves being held as contraband. The act also stated that slaves in Confederate territory would be freed if their owners were found to support the Confederacy. On July 17, 1862, Lincoln signed the bill into law.

JOHN P. PARKER

1827–1900

John P. Parker was born in Norfolk, Virginia, to a slave mother and a white father in 1827. When he was eight, Parker was sold south to Mobile, Alabama, where a doctor purchased him. Parker grew up with the doctor's family while enslaved as a domestic servant. When the doctor's sons learned to read and write, so did Parker, and when the doctor's sons headed north to attend college in 1843, Parker was sent as well. But the doctor worried Parker would escape and brought him back to Alabama to work at the foundry. Parker did try to escape during this time but was caught. Fearing he would be forced to accept work as a field hand, he moved to New Orleans with his owner's approval. He found work at a foundry there. By 1845 he had saved $1,800 and was able to buy his freedom.[4]

Parker moved to the Cincinnati area, where he began working as a conductor for the Underground Railroad. He helped many slaves escape to freedom. In 1854, Parker opened his own foundry in Ripley, Ohio. When the Civil War broke out in 1861, the foundry made parts for the Union war effort. Then, when the Union announced in 1863 that African Americans could serve in the Union army, Parker recruited soldiers for Ohio's Twenty-Seventh US Colored Infantry Regiment. Parker remained in the foundry business until his death in 1900 at the age of 73.

Parker's home is now a national historic landmark.

The promise of freedom caused many escaped slaves who had not made it into Free States to linger around Union army encampments, asking for food and work. But still, many of the freed slaves had no place to go, nothing to eat, and no source of income. It soon became clear that the influx of runaway slaves needed places to stay.

CONTRABAND CAMPS

In November 1862, Union general Ulysses S. Grant established the first contraband camp in Grand Junction, Tennessee. In the contraband camps, freed slaves received medical care, food, and a place to stay until they could find work and a more permanent home. Between the time the army established the first camp in 1862 and when the war ended in 1865, Union troops managed 100 contraband camps throughout the South.[5]

Life in the camps, however, was little better than conditions the former slaves left behind. In some cases, the camps were worse. African Americans often had to build their own shelters using whatever materials they could find. Cobbled together from sticks and stones, the shacks did nothing to keep out the chill when temperatures dropped. Without warm clothing, refugees were vulnerable to disease and illness, which quickly spread through the crowded, unsanitary camps. Between 1862 and 1870, diseases such as smallpox and cholera took the lives of 1 million of the 4 million slaves who had been freed during the war.[6]

Reports of the dire conditions in the camps caught the attention of Northern aid groups, including the Chicago Colored Ladies' Freedmen's Aid Society and the Contraband Relief Associations in Washington, DC, and Boston. These organizations gathered warm clothing, food, and soap, and delivered care packages to the camps. Northern black women who had once been slaves, including well-known abolitionists Sojourner Truth and Harriet Jacobs, traveled to the camps to help care for the refugees. Women from Northern aid groups and Christian organizations also volunteered to teach African Americans in the camps to read and write. These skills would give the former slaves a chance to find better jobs.

FINDING WORK

Former slaves living in the contraband camps wanted to find paying work and begin their lives as free people. Many offered to work for the Union troops, which in most cases welcomed the extra manpower. African-American men volunteered to build fortifications and

CORINTH CONTRABAND CAMP

Not all contraband camps had such poor conditions. Some, such as the Corinth Contraband Camp near Shiloh, Tennessee, were places that offered former slaves hope and opportunities. Established by Union general Grenville M. Dodge in 1862, Corinth consisted of sturdy homes, a school, a hospital, and a church. As part of a cooperative farm program, men and women worked in nearby fields, growing cotton and vegetables and selling the harvest for profit. Children attended school, where they learned to read and write. Through the services and support provided at Corinth, 1,000 adults and children learned to read, and 6,000 former slaves successfully transitioned from slavery to freedom.[7]

dig trenches for the Union army. Women offered to launder and mend soldiers' clothing, nurse those who were wounded in battle, and grow and prepare food. Many African Americans offered to spy for the Union as well.

As Union troops took over Confederate territories where cotton plantations stood, the federal government hired former slaves to harvest and plant the crops. Plantation owners who were loyal to the Union also hired those who were living in contraband camps. But in both instances, the African-American

AFRICAN-AMERICAN SPIES

During the Civil War, African-American men and women were in a unique position to gather information in the South. The culture of slavery allowed black men and women to move among Confederate leaders virtually unnoticed. William A. Jackson was a slave who labored as Confederate president Jefferson Davis's coachman during the Civil War. In this position, Jackson was able to overhear Davis's conversations while traveling by coach. Mary Elizabeth Bowser was also enslaved in the Confederate capitol. She allegedly had a photographic memory and was able to accurately report the contents of documents she came across while enslaved. Jackson and Bowser both relayed their knowledge to the Union army.

Fugitive slaves provided the Union armies with valuable information on the movement of Confederate troops as well. Based on the information of one such slave, George Scott, Union general Benjamin F. Butler learned that Confederate forces were planning an attack on Newport News, Virginia. From that point forward, Butler ordered that all fugitive slaves escaping through Union-held territory be questioned. Oftentimes, the escaped slaves were more than willing to cooperate.

A group of contrabands contributes labor to a Union encampment in Yorkville, Virginia, in May 1862.

workers received meager pay for long days of hard work. By contrast, farther west, land seized by Union troops was sometimes distributed among recently freed slaves to begin farming. As African Americans who had been freed by the Second Confiscation Act struggled to start their lives as free citizens, abolitionists continued working to ensure the freedom of all those still enslaved in the Confederacy.

Lincoln presented the Emancipation Proclamation to his cabinet following a number of Union losses. He waited to announce it publicly until a Union victory

ABOLITIONISTS AND EMANCIPATION

Five days after President Lincoln signed the Second Confiscation Act into law, he prepared to make an even bigger move to free slaves. On July 22, 1862, Lincoln read a draft of the Emancipation Proclamation to his cabinet. The document promised freedom for slaves throughout the Confederacy, but Lincoln was not yet ready to issue the proclamation publicly.

Since the beginning of the Civil War, abolitionists had argued that the key to a Union victory was to free the slaves and allow African-American men to fight on the side of the Union. But Lincoln and other leaders within the federal government did not want to lose the border states to secession. These leaders held firmly to the belief that the Union was fighting to reunite the country, not to emancipate African-American slaves and bring an end to the institution of slavery. This was a constant source of frustration for abolitionists, who supported the president once he was elected but were unhappy when he appeared to drag his feet on the subject of opposing slavery.

For example, the Second Confiscation Act had given the Union army the authority to seize slaves of Confederate supporters in Union-controlled areas, but the policy was not being enforced, as it was difficult to tell to whom slaves belonged with their owners not present. Additionally, the act had given Lincoln the power to employ African Americans "in such manner as he may judge best

COLONIZATION

Many politicians in the North and South, including Lincoln, believed the solution to the issue of slavery was to move African Americans to a new colony in Liberia, Haiti, or South America. Hundreds of free blacks, weary of dealing with constant discrimination, decided to move to Haiti in 1861. But this was a small percentage of the free black population in the United States at that time.

Most Northern free blacks, including abolitionists, were angered by the idea. In Philadelphia, free blacks wrote an appeal to Lincoln: "Many of us have our own house and other property, amounting in the aggregate, to millions of dollars. Shall we sacrifice this, leave our homes, forsake our birthplace, and flee to a strange land, to appease the anger and prejudice of the traitors now in arms against the government?"[1] When the idea of colonization was finally dismissed in the early years of the war, abolitionists and free African Americans united behind the cause of emancipation.

The Second Confiscation Act allowed slaves to work as laborers for the Union, but Lincoln had not yet authorized them to enlist as soldiers.

for the public welfare," but Lincoln had not yet suggested blacks could fight for the Union.[2] Abolitionist Horace Greeley expressed abolitionists' frustration with the government's slow action on the issue of slavery in an article in the *New York Tribune* on August 19, 1862: "On the face of this wide earth, Mr. President, there is not one disinterested, determined, intelligent champion of the Union cause who does not feel that all attempts to put down the rebellion and at the same time uphold its inciting cause are preposterous and futile."[3]

ABOLITIONISTS

The Second Great Awakening, a religious movement that swept through the United States in the early 1800s, was based on the idea that people had the ability to take action to improve the world around them. In the 1830s, this era of social activism gave rise to the abolitionist movement, which preached about the evils of slavery and worked to end it. In 1831, William Lloyd Garrison, a prominent white abolitionist, began publishing the *Liberator*, an antislavery newspaper in Boston. Two years later, Theodore Weld, Arthur Tappan, and Lewis Tappan formed the American Anti-Slavery Society in Philadelphia. It worked to abolish slavery, spoke out against racial prejudice, and pledged to use nonviolent means to achieve its goals. Keeping this pledge was not always easy, as angry proslavery white mobs staged hostile protests at abolitionist events. Protesters burned abolitionist literature and sometimes even attacked the abolitionists.

Through articles that appeared in the *Liberator* and the many pamphlets printed by the Anti-Slavery Society and other groups, word spread and people joined the fight to end slavery. By 1835, the abolitionist movement was beginning to gain political traction as many new antislavery groups were established around the nation. Free blacks and those who had recently escaped from slavery began to attend meetings, gather supplies for freed slaves, and sometimes lend a hand on the Underground Railroad. In the early 1840s, former slaves and abolitionists Frederick Douglass and Sojourner Truth traveled around the country with William Lloyd Garrison, speaking at abolitionist meetings and rallies. By speaking about their own experiences with slavery and by writing about their lives as slaves in memoirs, Douglass and Truth were able to convince many to join the abolitionist movement.

Wendell Phillips gives a speech on slavery in Boston. Abolitionists such as Phillips often held public gatherings to talk about slavery.

Finally, on September 22, following a narrow but significant Union victory at the Battle of Antietam, Lincoln issued a preliminary version of his Emancipation Proclamation, which said all slaves in the Confederate-controlled states would become free if the Confederacy did not surrender by January 1, 1863.

A NEW PURPOSE

One hundred days after the initial announcement, on the first day of the year, the Emancipation Proclamation officially went into effect. For black abolitionist Frederick Douglass and other prominent leaders of the abolitionist movement, it was a day they would never forget. Douglass, who celebrated the momentous occasion in Boston with abolitionist friends William Wells Brown and J. Sella Martin, said, "We shout for joy that we live to record this righteous decree."[4]

All across the North, African Americans gathered together for jubilant celebrations. Hundreds of African Americans congregated outside the White

KEEPING A SECRET

When the Emancipation Proclamation was signed, slaves in the most rural parts of the South did not find out about it right away. Slave owners in the South did not tell their slaves about the proclamation. They did not want their slaves to leave their property. As a result, many slaves continued working for months before they heard through slaves from other plantations that they were legally free. Finally, the federal government sent undercover agents into the South to inform the slaves that they were now free. In one case, a slave claimed to have not heard until 1864, more than a year after the proclamation was in effect.

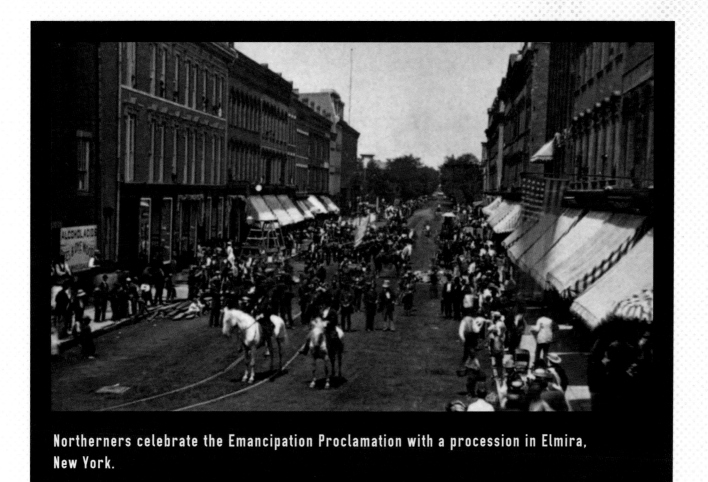

Northerners celebrate the Emancipation Proclamation with a procession in Elmira, New York.

House in Washington, DC, celebrating the emancipation. A celebrant at an event in Harrisburg, Pennsylvania, wrote, "We, the Colored Citizens of the city of Harrisburg, hail this first day of January, 1863, as a new era in our country's history—a day in which injustice and oppression were forced to flee and cower before the benign principles of justice and righteousness."[5]

The Emancipation Proclamation did more than promise freedom to slaves in the Confederacy; the proclamation also shifted the North's purpose for fighting the war. Instead of fighting only to preserve the Union, the motive Lincoln had insisted upon from the start of the war, the Union began fighting to abolish slavery throughout the Confederacy. Additionally, the proclamation announced Lincoln's new view on what it meant to employ African Americans in a way that was "best for the public welfare."[6] The document opened the door for black men to become Union soldiers. Finally, the time had come for African Americans to join the fight for freedom.

RECRUITING AFRICAN AMERICANS FOR THE UNION

Abolitionists such as Douglass, Henry Highland Garnet, and Mary Ann Shadd Cary wasted no time spreading the word that the Union army was now open to African Americans to fight as soldiers. They worked to recruit soldiers in the North for the Union army, traveling thousands of miles, speaking at rallies, and appearing at recruitment events. Posters announcing "Freedom, Protection, Pay, and a Call to Military Duty!" were plastered on walls around Northern cities and towns.[7] Recruiting advertisements appeared in African-American newspapers and magazines.

Douglass met with government leaders, wrote letters to powerful friends, and wrote articles in his newspaper appealing to young blacks to take up arms for the

FREDERICK DOUGLASS

c. 1818–1895

Frederick Augustus Washington Bailey was born a slave in Talbot County, Maryland, in approximately 1818. Bailey lived with his grandmother and seldom saw his mother, who died when he was approximately ten years old. Bailey was sent to Baltimore, Maryland, to live in the home of Hugh and Sophia Auld, where he learned to read. When Bailey was 16, the Aulds sent him to live with Edward Covey, a slave owner who had a reputation for beating slaves. Covey beat Bailey often, nearly breaking his spirit, but Bailey eventually fought back in a fistfight. Covey never beat him again.

Bailey escaped from slavery with the help of Anna Murray, a free black woman he loved. Bailey and Murray married and settled in New Bedford, Massachusetts. Bailey changed his last name to Douglass.

Douglass began attending church and abolitionist meetings, where he met William Lloyd Garrison. Douglass told his story to the group so eloquently that Garrison invited him to be a regular speaker. Garrison also convinced Douglass to write the story of his life as a slave. Douglass's book, *My Bondage and My Freedom*, was published in 1855. In December 1847, Douglass began to publish his own antislavery newspaper, the *North Star*.

When the Civil War began, Douglass advised Lincoln to emancipate the slaves and allow them to fight in the Union army. After the war, Douglass remained a strong advocate for human rights. Douglass died on February 20, 1895.

Union. In "Men of Color, to Arms!" an article Douglass published in his paper in March 1863, he extended his first invitation for black men to join the Union army. The request drummed up more than 100 men from upstate New York, who reported to boot camp for the Fifty-Fourth Massachusetts soon after.[8]

On July 6, 1863, Douglass was one of three speakers at a meeting promoting the African-American enlistments at National Hall in Philadelphia. That evening, Douglass encouraged African-American men to join the Union army. If they did, Douglass himself promised they would gain full citizenship. He did not know this to be true at the time, but he hoped it would be possible once the Union won the war. Douglass said, "Once let the black man get upon his person the brass letters *US*, let him get an eagle on his button, and a musket on his shoulder and bullets in his pockets, and there is no power on Earth which can deny that he has earned the right of citizenship in the United States."[9]

While Douglass rounded up men in New York and in other Northern states, Sojourner Truth did her part to recruit soldiers in Michigan, where she lived. Truth even penned a song called "The Valiant Soldiers" for the First Michigan Colored Regiment, which she sang for audiences in Detroit and Washington, DC, to the tune of the "Battle Hymn of the Republic." Truth's grandson, James Caldwell, was one of many she recruited. Caldwell went on to serve with the Fifty-Fourth Massachusetts.

SOJOURNER TRUTH

c. 1797–1883

Isabella Bomefree was born enslaved to a Dutch family in the Hudson valley of New York, in approximately 1797. When she was nine, she was sold with a flock of sheep for $100. After being sold to several different owners, in 1826 she escaped with her baby daughter. She took refuge in the home of the nearby Van Wagenen family and adopted their surname.

On July 4, 1827, New York voted to abolish slavery. The next year, Isabella won a court case against a white man for illegally selling her son into slavery. Her son was returned, and it was the first time a black woman won a lawsuit against a white man in the United States.

In 1843, Isabella officially changed her name to Sojourner Truth. A devout Methodist, she dedicated her life to the abolitionist cause. She joined the Northampton Association of Education and Industry, a community founded by abolitionists. Here Truth met Douglass, William Lloyd Garrison, and other well-known abolitionists. As the abolitionist movement grew in the mid-1850s, Truth turned her attention to public speaking. In her powerful speeches, she used examples from her own experiences to make her case against slavery.

When the Civil War broke out, Truth shared her story with President Lincoln, urging him to abolish slavery. She also gathered supplies for black soldiers and volunteered at contraband camps. After the war, Truth became a strong advocate for African-American rights, working to secure land for blacks.

Recruiters used illustrated portraits to get the word out about newly forming

SOLDIERS ON THE FRONT LINES

Soon after the Emancipation Proclamation had passed, Massachusetts's governor, John Andrew, contacted Secretary of War Edwin Stanton to request permission to recruit an all-black unit. Andrew, himself an abolitionist, was backed by funding from many prominent abolitionists in the North. Yet there was still strong opposition to the idea of African Americans fighting in the war. Andrew did not want to give the government time to reconsider the issue.

Andrew sent out the call for troops in early February 1863. But Massachusetts was home to few African Americans—only 75 men had responded by the end of the first week. Andrew extended the recruitment base to include all of the Northern and Southern states plus Canada, where many former slaves had gone to live after escaping. By the end of May 1863, 1,007 had enlisted, including many men from New York, Indiana, and Ohio.[1] Though some were as young as 16 years old, the regiment had enough enlistees to go to war.

On May 28, 1863, the Fifty-Fourth Massachusetts lined up in Boston Common, a park in downtown Boston, before heading south to Charleston, South Carolina. Thirty-seven white officers led the regiment, despite Governor Andrew's assertions that African-American men were perfectly capable of leading the troops. Bostonians and abolitionists, including Douglass, Wendell Phillips, and William Lloyd Garrison, came to see the regiment off and wish them well. In a parting statement, Andrew said, "I know not where in all human history to any given thousand men in arms there has been committed a work at once so proud, so precious, so full of hope and glory as the work committed to you."[2]

Although the Fifty-Fourth suffered a devastating defeat during their first major battle at Fort Wagner, the regiment went on to bravely fight in several battles throughout South Carolina, Georgia, and Florida over the next two years. The courageous demonstrations of the Fifty-Fourth Massachusetts and unofficial black regiments such as the First Louisiana and the First Kansas Colored Volunteer Infantry prompted more African-American regiments to form in the North and South. The US government had recently created the Bureau

John Andrew's widespread recruiting helped gather the 1,000 men needed to

PROVING THEMSELVES

Union generals hesitated to send black troops into battle, worrying they lacked the experience and bravery to go to war. But one battle at a time, black soldiers proved themselves on the front lines. On May 27, 1863, at Port Hudson, Louisiana, for example, the First and Third Louisiana Native Guard were part of the Union attack. Both of these all-black regiments had originally formed to support Louisiana Confederates, but had immediately changed sides once New Orleans came under Union control. The two regiments fought hard and proved their bravery at Port Hudson, sustaining 600 casualties.[4]

African-American soldiers continued to prove themselves in battles for the Union. Another important moment came on September 29, 1864, when three USCT regiments led the charge against Confederate defenses outside of the South's capital, Richmond, Virginia. During the Battle of New Market Heights, the black regiments sustained approximately 800 casualties in one hour, but they overtook the enemy line.[5] Fourteen black soldiers were awarded the Medal of Honor for their actions during the battle.

of Colored Troops. The bureau made unofficial regiments officially part of the Union army and organized and managed new African-American regiments. The African-American regiments were called United States Colored Troops (USCT). Eventually, African Americans comprised 163 regiments, while approximately 18,000 additional African Americans served in the navy.[3]

INGRAINED PREJUDICE

African Americans who served in the Union military faced prejudice at nearly every turn. They endured substandard wages, medical care, and training, and constantly had to prove themselves on the battlefield.

When African Americans were first recruited at the beginning of 1863, the federal government promised them equal pay. In June 1863, however, Lincoln

AFRICAN AMERICANS IN THE NAVY

From the very beginning of the war, black sailors were allowed to join the navy, where they had served since the 1840s as boat pilots, coal heavers, shipboard firemen, and stewards. Recruitment was initially limited to freemen, who would serve as cooks and assistant gunners. But in 1862, all positions were opened to blacks after disease took many white sailors out of service. An estimated 18,000 African Americans served in the Union navy, comprising approximately 20 percent of the total force.[6] Black sailors served with white sailors in fully integrated environments. A total of 800 black sailors died during battles, while more than 2,000 died from diseases.[7] Although ships were integrated, African Americans faced a great deal of racism and hazing from white sailors. Only 0.6 percent of African-American sailors were promoted to officer during the Civil War.[8]

went back on this promise. He said African-American soldiers were technically employed under the Militia Act of 1862, which Congress had passed on the same day as the Second Confiscation Act. Because the Militia Act defined black recruits as laborers, they would be paid laborers' wages. Regardless of rank, black Union soldiers made ten dollars per month with three dollars deducted for uniforms. A white private made 13 dollars per month with no such deduction.

Black soldiers reacted in a variety of ways to this injustice. Some simply refused to enlist at all. Soldiers of the Fifty-Fourth Massachusetts protested unequal wages by serving a year without pay. Even after the Massachusetts state government offered to make up the difference, black soldiers refused to accept

Despite facing the same risks as white soldiers, African-American soldiers received less money until June 1864.

it. As one soldier stated, "We did not come to fight for money . . . [but for the principle] that made us men when we enlisted."[9]

In November 1863, a man named William Walker took more drastic measures. Walker was a sergeant in the Third Regiment South Carolina Volunteer Infantry of the Union army. He refused to work in order to protest low pay of African

Americans, and he convinced others to follow him. While the regiment was in Jacksonville, Florida, they resigned from the army. The strike called attention to the plight of African-American soldiers in the Union army and prompted Stanton to call for equal pay for all soldiers, black and white. Although Walker was shot for mutiny in February 1864, a law was passed in June 1864 that granted equal pay for African-American soldiers, and many were also able to earn back pay.

Black soldiers also encountered many other forms of racism. Most white officers did not believe African Americans were capable of leading their own troops, so few were promoted to the rank of officer. By the war's end, only 100 black officers had been commissioned.[10]

Many of the white officers that commanded black troops were prejudiced themselves. As a result, they denied the men in their regiments proper training, leaving them vulnerable during battle. White soldiers often treated black soldiers as second-class citizens as well. For example, in Saltville, Virginia, on October 2, 1864, white Union troops were verbally abusive to colored Union troops when going into battle.

Black soldiers often received the assignments no other soldiers wanted, such as burial duty or the grueling, never-ending work of digging trenches and building fortifications. If a black Union soldier was captured or otherwise left to the mercy of Confederate troops, he could expect to be executed on the spot, sent to prison camps, or brought to Southern slaveholders. If a white commanding

FORT PILLOW MASSACRE

After a tough defeat in March 1864, Confederate cavalry forces under the direction of Nathan Bedford Forrest sought revenge. On April 12, they attacked Union troops at the weakly defended Fort Pillow in Tennessee. Union troops numbered only one-third of the Confederate soldiers and included 262 black soldiers.[11] After the Union surrendered, the Confederates continued shooting. Black and white Union soldiers tried to get away but were killed as they fled. The *New York Herald* ran a story titled, "Massacre of White and Black Troops, Women and Children Murdered in Cold Blood, The dead and Wounded Negroes Burned." The story described the massacre:

Both white and black were bayoneted, shot, or sabred. Even dead bodies were horribly mutilated and children of seven and eight years and several Negro women killed in cold blood. Soldiers unable to speak from wounds were shot dead and their bodies rolled down the banks into the river. The dead and wounded Negroes were piled in heaps and burned, and several citizens who had joined our forces for protection were killed or wounded.[12]

The senseless killings at Fort Pillow deeply affected many black soldiers, who swore they would take revenge. "Remember Fort Pillow" became a rallying cry for African-American regiments.

officer of black troops fell into Confederate hands, he too was often killed. When a white commanding officer of an all-white troop was captured, on the other hand, he was taken prisoner. The discrimination African-American soldiers experienced in regiment camps and on the battlefield was a direct reflection of the prejudice that continued to exist against blacks, whether they were enslaved or free, living in the North or South.

CARTE DE VISITE

Although photography was a relatively new invention when the Civil War began in 1861, cartes de visite, or pocket-sized keepsake photos, were very popular. As soldiers headed off to war, they often had photos taken of themselves in uniform to leave behind with family members. By the same token, soldiers also carried small photos of their family members with them into battle. Soldiers would pull these photos from a pocket when they were feeling bored or lonely to remind them of loved ones back home. There are many stories of soldiers asking for their family photos when they were dying, or of dead soldiers found on the battlefield with a carte de visite of a spouse or child clutched in one hand.

Once African-American soldiers were finally able to join the army in 1863, many had a photo taken in uniform. These cartes de visite were especially meaningful to African-American families, as they were living proof their soldier had been recognized as a man and a member of the United States. Such an acknowledgment was a step forward for black Americans, who up to this point had been denied such status.

Carte de visite of John Sharper, a member of the Fourteenth Rhode Island Heavy
Artillery Regiment

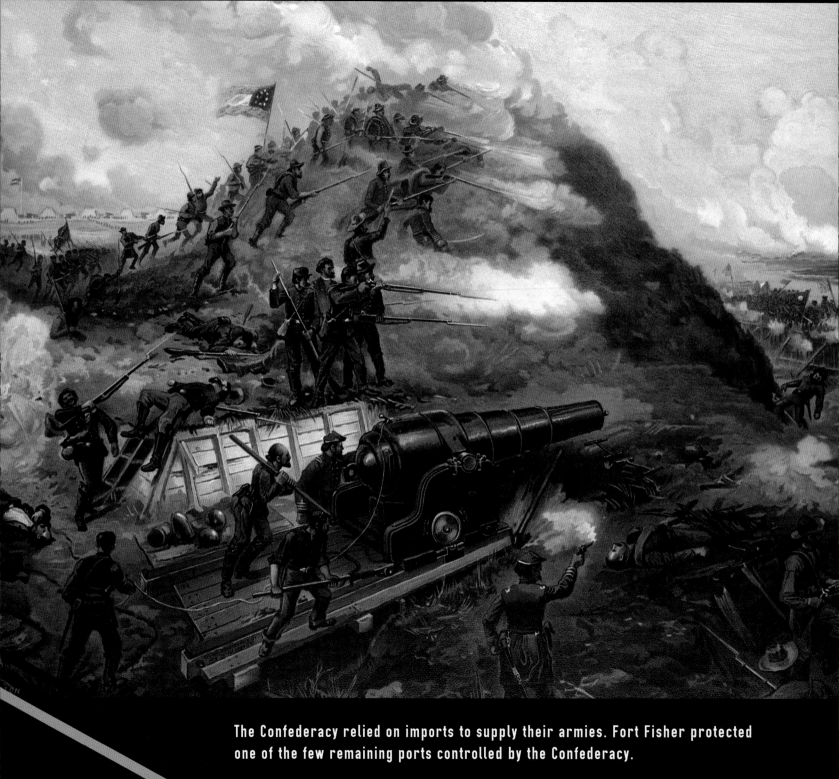

The Confederacy relied on imports to supply their armies. Fort Fisher protected one of the few remaining ports controlled by the Confederacy.

SURRENDER AND RECONSTRUCTION

In January 1865, things were not looking good for the Confederacy, even though Confederate president Jefferson Davis remained optimistic. Union general William T. Sherman's troops marched to South Carolina, facing little to no opposition from the Confederates along the way. Fort Fisher, a Confederate stronghold that protected a vital trade route in North Carolina, fell to Union forces on January 15. In February, Davis offered to discuss peace with Lincoln on terms that allowed the South to remain independent. Lincoln rejected the proposal. In the meantime, Southern troops were existing on meager rations and beginning to desert.

As African Americans helped push the Union army toward victory, abolitionists continued to fight for more rights for blacks. Although the Emancipation Proclamation had freed slaves in the Confederate states, slavery still existed in the border states of Delaware, Missouri, Kentucky, and Maryland. In addition, many laws restricting the freedom of African Americans in the North and South still existed. There was still much to do.

Douglass led the effort, meeting often with Lincoln, writing articles to push for human rights for African Americans and speaking to audiences at abolitionist meetings throughout the North. Truth met with the president as well, sharing her personal story and thoughts on freedom. As a result of abolitionist persistence, the US Congress passed the Thirteenth Amendment on January 31, 1865. When ratified nearly one year later, it would effectively abolish slavery.

On April 9, 1865, a few months after the Thirteenth Amendment had passed, Robert E. Lee, general-in-chief of the Confederate armies, surrendered to Union commanding general Ulysses S. Grant at Appomattox Court House, Virginia. At long last, the devastating Civil War had come to an end. Parades and celebrations erupted in the streets of Northern cities, while many Southern cities were in shambles. Lincoln began to devise a plan to repair and reconstruct the torn nation.

After abandoning Richmond, Virginia, on April 1 and being unable to meet up with additional troops, Lee had no choice but to surrender his army on April 9, 1865.

But within days of the war's end, tragedy struck. Late on the evening of April 14, 1865, shots rang out at Ford's Theatre in Washington, DC. Lincoln had been watching a play at the theater when an actor and Confederate sympathizer, John Wilkes Booth, slipped into Lincoln's viewing box and shot him. At 7:22 a.m. the next morning, the president was pronounced dead. Overnight, the celebratory mood that had swept through the North following the Civil War victory faded to somber mourning for the president. The future of the still-unstable Union was uncertain.

A NEW PRESIDENT

Upon Lincoln's death, Vice President Andrew Johnson stepped in as president for the remainder of Lincoln's term. Lincoln's plan for the reconstruction of the nation had not been unveiled before the time of his death. But in a speech three days before the shooting, Lincoln had stated that his plans for reconstruction in the state of Louisiana included granting the right to vote to free blacks and those who had served in the Union army. Lincoln's statement implied the federal government would have had some control over reconstruction in individual states. But President Johnson, a Southerner who had just been sworn in as Lincoln's vice president six weeks earlier, had a different plan.

In May 1865, Johnson shared his ideas for reconstruction. Under Johnson's plan, all states, including those in the South, would govern themselves, with

40 ACRES AND A MULE

Immediately after the war, Union general William T. Sherman arranged to give 40,000 black families 40 acres and a mule so they could begin to provide for themselves as free individuals. The plan, approved by Lincoln and known as Sherman's Field Order Number 15, declared that the plots of land, located along a strip of coast between Charleston and the Saint John's River in Florida, were to exist as a settlement for African Americans. But when Johnson became president, he repealed the order and gave all land back to the previous plantation owners. The Anti-Slavery Society and other abolitionists demanded land for African Americans. Sojourner Truth worked to secure land grants for freed slaves in the South. With land of their own to farm, Truth and other abolitionists argued, African Americans had an opportunity to become self-sufficient. Although she fought long and hard for the land ownership program, Truth was unable to convince the US Congress of the merits of the plan.

little direction from the federal government. This meant that under Johnson, the federal establishment of voting requirements that Lincoln had mentioned in his speech would be left up to the individual states.

Johnson's reconstruction policies strongly favored the pro-Union white elite in the South who had backed the Confederacy once the war began. Under Johnson, all Southern land that had been given to freed slaves by the federal government during the war was returned to previous white landowners, putting wealth and power back into the hands of the Southern aristocracy. This policy made progress difficult for the Freedmen's Bureau, a government agency created near the end of the war to help ease slaves' transitions to freedom.

State policies also threatened to roll back many of the civil rights gains blacks had achieved during the war. Southern states passed Black Code laws, which prevented African Americans from getting certain jobs. With little land and few opportunities, many Southern blacks turned to fieldwork. In a system known as sharecropping, Southern blacks in need of jobs lived on the land and farmed the fields for white landowners, who needed a workforce.

FREEDMEN'S BUREAU

In March 1865, Congress launched the Bureau of Refugees, Freedmen, and Abandoned Lands, also known as the Freedmen's Bureau. The bureau's main goal was to help blacks and whites in the South adjust to life after slavery. Under the direction of the US War Department and managed by Civil War Union general Oliver O. Howard, the bureau monitored the operation of 3,000 schools for free blacks; attempted to settle blacks on abandoned land; provided food, shelter, and medical assistance to poor blacks and whites; settled disputes between landowners and black tenants; and helped ensure that blacks were treated fairly in Southern courts of law.[1] The Freedmen's Bureau disbanded in 1872, having created several colleges and training schools for blacks, one of which was Howard University. But the Freedmen's Bureau made little progress bridging the gap between whites and blacks in the South, mainly because the organization had little support from politicians in the North or the South.

NORTHERN BACKLASH

Republicans in the North reacted strongly to Johnson's reconstruction plan. Fueled by the desire to veto Johnson's pro-Southern policies, Northern voters overwhelmingly elected Republican candidates to Congress in the 1866 elections. These new congressmen were

able to redirect Johnson's plan for reconstruction, granting more rights to African Americans.

Congress began by passing the Civil Rights Act of 1866 and the Reconstruction Acts of 1867. The Civil Rights Act granted legal citizenship and equal rights to all men in the United States, regardless of the color of their skin. The Reconstruction Acts of 1867 established five military districts in the South in which federal soldiers were stationed to keep the peace and ensure that Southerners complied with civil rights laws. The acts also set up a state government system in which officials were elected by both black and white male voters. In addition to limiting the voting rights of officials who served the Confederate government and preventing them from running for office in the postwar South, the acts granted male African Americans the right to run for public office. And, in order to be readmitted into the Union, the Reconstruction Acts required Southern states to ratify the Fourteenth Amendment, which granted citizenship to anyone born in the United States, including recently freed slaves. The amendment went into effect on July 9, 1868.

AFRICAN AMERICANS IN OFFICE

With the passage of the Reconstruction Acts, African Americans were elected to public office in Southern states and to US Congress for the first time. For many within the black community who had recently become active in newly formed chapters of the Equal Rights League and other civil rights groups throughout the South, this was the moment they had waited for. The countless hours spent in meetings, petitioning, protesting, and speaking up at state and local conventions had paid off.

As a result of their efforts and thanks to the passing of the Fifteenth Amendment on February 3, 1870, which granted African-American men the right to vote, approximately 2,000 black citizens won election to local, state, and federal government offices. One hundred of those elected were former slaves. In all, 16 African Americans were elected to Congress, including Hiram Revels, who

CARPETBAGGERS AND SCALAWAGS

After the war, Northern whites headed south to purchase abandoned plantation lands. Middle-class teachers, shopkeepers, businessmen, soldiers, or Freedmen's Bureau employees also headed south. These people wanted to help reform and rebuild the South and assist newly freed blacks. Southerners referred to all Northerners who arrived in the years following the war as *carpetbaggers*, a derogatory term referring to the luggage the newcomers brought with them.

Southerners also used the term *scalawag* to label Southerners who voted for the Republican Party and supported the federal government reforms during Reconstruction. Most scalawags were merchants, non-slave-owning farmers, or other middle-class Southerners who were loyal to the Union during the war. Wealthy planters from the Lower South who supported equal rights for blacks were called scalawags, too. During Reconstruction, African Americans, carpetbaggers, and scalawags formed a Republican voting coalition in the South. With the help of this voting coalition, many African Americans were voted into office between 1867 and 1869.

Hiram Revels was the first African American elected to the US Senate.

won a seat in the Senate representing Mississippi, the same seat Jefferson Davis, president of the Confederacy, had once occupied.[2]

THE RISE OF WHITE SUPREMACY

But African Americans quickly realized that in their case, winning elections did not necessarily lead to political power and greater equality. Instead, the elections made some Southern whites angry enough to seek revenge, doing anything they could to regain power. Many of these people were white supremacists. They believed African Americans were not as good as white people. White supremacists formed organizations such as the Ku Klux Klan (KKK) to intimidate, terrorize, and sometimes kill blacks who posed a threat to their desired social order.

Between 1868 and 1871, white supremacist groups strategically targeted black leaders, blacks who tried to vote, and blacks who attempted to get an education. White supremacist groups murdered at least 35 African Americans who were elected to public office during this time.[3] White supremacists also teamed up with Southern Democrats in leadership positions and used fraud and violence to make sure more blacks did not get elected to public office.

LOOKING AHEAD TO THE FUTURE

In the decade following the Civil War, African Americans experienced great ups and downs. As a result of the war, African Americans had gained freedom from the threat of slavery and earned citizenship under the law. Black men had gained the right to vote, and with the support of Republicans in the North and South, a significant number of African Americans were elected to public office for the first time.

The Ku Klux Klan was founded in 1866. Members worked to terrorize African Americans and resist Reconstruction-era policies.

Yet many whites in the South and in the North still treated African Americans as second-class citizens. In the North, prejudice prevented African Americans from getting well-paying jobs and otherwise fitting into society. Many Southern whites resisted the new civil rights laws with all their might, enacting Black Codes to restrict the behavior and employment options of blacks.

White supremacist organizations such as the KKK used violence and hate speech to intimidate Southern blacks and any whites who tried to help them. For many blacks in the South, life improved very little from 1865 through the late 1800s because of KKK lynchings, killings, and harassment.

But through years of involvement in the abolitionist movement, in civic organizations such as black Masonic lodges, and in civil rights organizations such as the Equal Rights League, African-American communities became more influential. Eventually, the equal rights they had fought so hard for in the Civil War would be theirs, but in the meantime, African Americans faced a long, uphill battle. It would not be until the civil rights movement of the 1960s that blacks would begin to earn equal rights under the law.

NATIONAL EQUAL RIGHTS LEAGUE

In 1864, abolitionists Henry Highland Garnet, Frederick Douglass, and John Mercer Langston founded the National Equal Rights League (NERL). The organization worked to gain full citizenship for all African-American men who served as Union troops in the Civil War. Once the war ended, local Equal Rights League chapters formed in states throughout the nation, including Louisiana, Michigan, Pennsylvania, Massachusetts, Ohio, Missouri, and North Carolina. These postwar leagues focused their efforts on supporting Republican policies and promoting civil rights in their communities. Pennsylvania chapters successfully pushed to end segregation on streetcars in 1866, while the league's Cleveland, Ohio, chapter lobbied unsuccessfully to integrate schools. In later years, NERL supported women's rights. By the early 1900s, many NERL members left to join the National Association for the Advancement of Colored People (NAACP), which allowed anyone to join, regardless of skin color.

TIMELINE

April 12, 1861

Confederate troops attack Fort Sumter, near Charleston, South Carolina, igniting the Civil War.

August 6, 1861

The First Confiscation Act is passed, allowing slaves who worked for the Confederacy to be seized as contraband.

November 1861

Harriet Tubman makes her last trip to the South with the Underground Railroad to guide escaping slaves to freedom in the North.

July 17, 1862

The Second Confiscation Act is passed, allowing free blacks or slaves to be employed by the Union army.

July 18, 1863

The Fifty-Fourth Massachusetts Regiment leads the attack on Fort Wagner near Charleston, South Carolina.

April 12, 1864

Confederate forces attack Fort Pillow, Tennessee, killing soldiers, women, and children.

January 31, 1865

The Thirteenth Amendment is passed, abolishing slavery in the United States.

April 9, 1865

Robert E. Lee surrenders to Ulysses S. Grant at Appomattox Court House, Virginia, ending the Civil War.

July 13, 1863

Rioters in New York City target free African Americans during a draft riot.

November 1862

Union general Ulysses S. Grant establishes the first contraband camp for freed slaves in Grand Junction, Tennessee.

January 1, 1863

President Abraham Lincoln signs the Emancipation Proclamation.

February 1863

Massachusetts governor John Andrew calls for African Americans to enlist in the Union army.

April 14, 1865

John Wilkes Booth, a Confederate sympathizer, assassinates Lincoln at Ford's Theatre in Washington, DC.

May 1865

President Andrew Johnson unveils plans for Reconstruction that would return power to white planters.

July 9, 1868

The Fourteenth Amendment goes into effect, granting citizenship to all born in the United States.

February 3, 1870

The Fifteenth Amendment is ratified, granting African-American men the right to vote.

ESSENTIAL FACTS

KEY PLAYERS

- Frederick Douglass was a leading abolitionist who helped pressure Lincoln to emancipate slaves and allow blacks to join the Union army.

- John P. Parker was a free black man and conductor on the Underground Railroad. He helped shepherd approximately 1,000 slaves across the Ohio River to freedom. During the war, he recruited soldiers for Ohio's Twenty-Seventh US Colored Troops Regiment.

- Sojourner Truth was an active abolitionist and women's rights advocate. She recruited black soldiers in Michigan and met with Lincoln to share her views on slavery. After the war, Truth lobbied for the US Congress to grant land to freed slaves.

- Harriet Tubman escaped from slavery and became a well-known conductor on the Underground Railroad. She made 19 trips into the South to rescue 70 slaves.

KEY STATISTICS

- 488,070 free blacks lived in the North and South in 1860.

- Between 1862 and 1865, Union troops managed 100 contraband camps.

- Between 1862 and 1870, 1 million of 4 million freed slaves died from diseases.

- 180,000 African Americans fought for the Union army; 18,000 served in the navy.

- 36,000 African Americans died in combat for the Union army.

- 2,000 African Americans were elected to local, state, and federal positions in February 1869.

IMPACT ON WAR

Thanks in large part to the bravery of the 180,000 black soldiers who volunteered to fight for the Union army after emancipation in 1863, the Union was able to win the war. Many African Americans risked their lives to spy for the North, slipping back into Confederate territory for the sole purpose of gathering information for the Union army, shifting the war in the North's favor. Many other African Americans worked in Northern factories, producing supplies for the war effort.

QUOTE

"Once let the black man get upon his person the brass letters *US*, let him get an eagle on his button, and a musket on his shoulder and bullets in his pockets, and there is no power on Earth which can deny that he has earned the right of citizenship in the United States."

—*Frederick Douglass*

GLOSSARY

ABOLITIONIST
A person who wants to end slavery.

BORDER STATE
A state that was located on the border between the Union and the Confederacy.

CABINET
The president's key advisers.

CASUALTY
A person who is injured, missing, or killed during a military campaign.

COALITION
A collection of groups or people that have joined together for a common purpose.

CONFEDERACY
The states that seceded from the United States to form the Confederate States of America.

DISCRIMINATION
Unfair treatment of other people, usually because of race, age, or gender.

EMANCIPATION
The act of freeing an individual or group from slavery.

LYNCHING
The act of illegally killing a person through mob action.

PREJUDICE
An opinion that is not based on reason or actual experience.

RAMPART
A wall or embankment built to protect against attack.

REGIMENT
An army unit typically commanded by a colonel.

REPUBLICAN
A member of the political party formed to oppose the spread of slavery in the United States.

SECESSION
The formal withdrawal of one group or region from a political union.

SEGREGATION
The practice of separating groups of people based on race, gender, ethnicity, or other factors.

UNION
States that remained loyal to the US government during the Civil War.

WHITE SUPREMACY
The belief that white people are superior to all other races.

ADDITIONAL RESOURCES

SELECTED BIBLIOGRAPHY

Claxton, Melvin, and Mark Puls. *Uncommon Valor: A Story of Race, Patriotism, and Glory in the Final Battles of the Civil War*. Hoboken, NJ: Wiley, 2006. Print.

Jenkins, Wilbert L. *Climbing Up to Glory: A Short History of African Americans during the Civil War and Reconstruction*. Wilmington, DE: Scholarly Resources, 2002. Print.

Kantrowitz, Stephen. *More Than Freedom: Fighting for Black Citizenship in a White Republic, 1829–1889*. New York: Penguin, 2012. Print.

FURTHER READINGS

Bolden, Tonya. *Emancipation Proclamation: Lincoln and the Dawn of Liberty*. New York: Abrams, 2013. Print.

Cummings, Judy Dodge. *Civil War*. Minneapolis: Abdo, 2014. Print.

Fradin, Judith Bloom, and Dennis Brindell Fradin. *Stolen into Slavery: The True Story of Solomon Northrup, Free Black Man.* Washington, DC: National Geographic Children's, 2014. Print.

WEBSITES

To learn more about Essential Library of the Civil War, visit **booklinks.abdopublishing.com**. These links are routinely monitored and updated to provide the most current information available.

PLACES TO VISIT

Corinth Contraband Camp
Shiloh National Military Park
1055 Pittsburg Landing Road
Shiloh, TN 38376
731-689-5696
http://www.nps.gov/shil/planyourvisit/contrabandcamp.htm
Located near the Shiloh battlefield, a memorial dedicated to the Corinth Contraband Camp includes bronze statues and a walkway.

Frederick Douglass National Historic Site
National Park Service
1411 W Street SE
Washington, DC 20020
202-426-5961
http://www.nps.gov/frdo/index.htm
Visit and tour the historic home of Frederick Douglass in Washington, DC, where he lived from 1878 until his death in 1895. The house is still filled with Douglass's furniture, books, and personal items.

Underground Railroad Historic Sites
http://www.nps.gov/nr/travel/underground/states.htm
Go to this site to learn more about Underground Railroad sites around the country that are open for tours. Specific links to sites with tour hours and history are included.

SOURCE NOTES

CHAPTER 1. THE BATTLE FOR FREEDOM BEGINS

1. "The 54th Massachusetts Infantry." *History.com*. A&E Television Networks, 2010. Web. 10 Nov. 2015.

2. Brian C. Pohanka. "Fort Wagner and the 54th Massachusetts Volunteer Infantry." *America's Civil War Magazine*. Historynet.com, 12 June 2006. Web. 19 Oct. 2015.

3. Ibid.

4. Kai Wright. *Soldiers of Freedom: An Illustrated History of African Americans in the Armed Forces*. New York: Black Dog & Leventhal, 2002. Print. 87.

5. Brian C. Pohanka. "Fort Wagner and the 54th Massachusetts Volunteer Infantry." *America's Civil War Magazine*. Historynet.com, 12 June 2006. Web. 19 Oct. 2015.

6. William C. Kashatus. "America's Civil War: 54th Massachusetts Regiment." *History.net*, 12 June 2006. Web. 12 Jan. 2016.

7. Kai Wright. *Soldiers of Freedom: An Illustrated History of African Americans in the Armed Forces*. New York: Black Dog & Leventhal, 2002. Print. 87.

8. Ira Berlin, Joseph P. Reidy, and Leslie S. Rowland. *The Black Military Experience*. Cambridge, UK: Cambridge UP, 1982. *Google Book Search*, 7 Jan. 2016. Web. 12.

9. Guy Gugliotta. "New Estimate Raises CW Death Toll." *New York Times*. New York Times, 2 Apr. 2012. Web. 19 Oct. 2015.

10. Brigid Schulte. "Women Soldiers Fought, Bled, and Died in the Civil War, Then Were Forgotten." *Washington Post*. Washington Post, 29 Apr. 2013. Web. 19 Oct. 2015.

CHAPTER 2. SLAVERY IN THE SOUTH

1. James Curry. "Narrative of James Curry, a Fugitive Slave." *Liberator*, 10 Jan. 1840: 1. *North Carolina Digital History*. Web. 16 Nov. 2015.

2. Nicholas Boston. "The Slave Experience: Living Conditions." *PBS.org*. Educational Broadcasting Corporation, 2004. Web. 16 Nov. 2015.

CHAPTER 3. FREE AFRICAN AMERICANS IN THE SOUTH

1. Henry Louis Gates Jr. "Why Did Free Blacks Stay in the Old South?" *Root*. Graham Holdings Company, 14 July 2013. Web. 18 Nov. 2015.

2. Susanna Michele Lee. "Free Blacks during the Civil War." *Encyclopedia Virginia*. Virginia Foundation for the Humanities, 27 Oct. 2015. Web. 17 Nov. 2015.

3. John Stauffer. "Yes, There Were Black Confederates. Here's Why." *Root*. Graham Holdings Company, 20 Jan. 2015. Web. 2 Nov. 2015.

4. Ibid.

5. Ibid.

6. Ibid.

7. Ibid.

CHAPTER 4. FREE AFRICAN AMERICANS IN THE NORTH

1. "The Northern Migration." *In Motion: The African American Migration Experience*. New York Public Library, 2005. Web. 12 Nov. 2015.

2. Stephen Kantrowitz. *More Than Freedom: Fighting for Black Citizenship in a White Republic, 1829-1889*. New York: Penguin, 2012. Print. 17.

3. "Timeline: African Americans in the Civil War." *PBS.org*. WGBH Educational Foundation, 2013. Web. 13 Oct. 2015.

4. Robert C. Kennedy. "On This Day: How to Escape the Draft." *New York Times*. New York Times, 2001. Web. 13 Jan. 2016.

5. Ibid.

6. "Fugitive Slave Acts." *History.com*. A&E Television Networks, 2009. Web. 18 Nov. 2015.

CHAPTER 5. RUNAWAYS AND CONTRABAND

1. "Harriet Tubman." *Civil War Trust*. Civil War Trust, 2014. Web. 6 Oct. 2015.

2. Jim Knippenberg. "Railroad Conductors: Prominent Citizens Hid Slaves." *Cincinnati Enquirer*. Cincinnati.com, 1 Aug. 2004. Web. 16 Nov. 2015.

3. Ibid.

4. "John P. Parker, Abolitionist and Inventor." *African American Registry*. African American Registry, 2013. Web. 17 Nov. 2015.

5. "From Slaves to Contraband to Free People." *Boundless US History*. Boundless, 21 Jul. 2015. Web. 6 Nov. 2015.

6. Paul Harris. "How the End of Slavery Led to Starvation and Death for Millions of Black Americans." *Guardian*. Guardian News and Media Limited, 16 June 2012. Web. 6 Oct. 2015.

7. "Corinth Contraband Camp." *NPS.gov*. National Park Service, US Department of the Interior, 7 Feb. 2016. Web. 8 Feb. 2016.

SOURCE NOTES
CONTINUED

CHAPTER 6. ABOLITIONISTS AND EMANCIPATION

1. Wilbert L. Jenkins. *Climbing Up to Glory: A Short History of African Americans during the Civil War and Reconstruction.* Wilmington, DE: Scholarly Resources, 2002. Print. 13.

2. "The Second Confiscation Act." *Freedmen & Southern Society Project.* University of Maryland, 2016. Web. 29 Feb. 2016.

3. Horace Greeley. "The Prayer of Twenty Millions." *New York Tribune,* 19 Aug. 1862: 4. *The Abraham Lincoln Papers at the Library of Congress.* Web. 8 Feb. 2016.

4. Wilbert L. Jenkins. *Climbing Up to Glory: A Short History of African Americans during the Civil War and Reconstruction.* Wilmington, DE: Scholarly Resources, 2002. Print. 19.

5. Ibid. 18.

6. "The Second Confiscation Act." *Freedmen & Southern Society Project.* University of Maryland, 2016. Web. 29 Feb. 2016.

7. Elsie Freeman, Wynell Burroughs Schamel, and Jean West. "The Fight for Equal Rights: A Recruiting Poster for Black Soldiers in the Civil War." *Social Education* 56.2 (1992): 118–120. Print.

8. "Frederick Douglass, American Abolitionist." *AmericanCivilWar.com.* Central Design Lab, 5 June 2012. Web. 19 Nov. 2015.

9. Frederick Douglass. "Address at a Meeting for the Promotion of Colored Enlistments, Philadelphia." 6 July 1863. *Library of Congress.* Web. 19 Nov. 2015.

CHAPTER 7. SOLDIERS ON THE FRONT LINES

1. "The 54th Massachusetts Infantry." *History.com.* A&E Television Networks, 2010. Web. 10 Nov. 2015.

2. Ibid.

3. Joseph P. Reidy. "Black Men in Navy Blue During the Civil War." *Prologue* 33.3 (2001): n. pag. *NARA.* Web. 16 Oct. 2015.

4. "Port Hudson." *NPS.gov*. National Park Service, US Department of the Interior, 7 Feb. 2016. Web. 8 Feb. 2016.

5. "The Battle of New Market Heights." *NPS.gov*. National Park Service, US Department of the Interior, 7 Feb. 2016. Web. 8 Feb. 2016.

6. Joseph P. Reidy. "Black Men in Navy Blue During the Civil War." *Prologue* 33.3 (2001): n. pag. *NARA*. Web. 16 Oct. 2015.

7. Kai Wright. *Soldiers of Freedom: An Illustrated History of African Americans in the Armed Forces*. New York: Black Dog & Leventhal, 2002. Print. 84.

8. Joseph P. Reidy. "Black Men in Navy Blue During the Civil War." *Prologue* 33.3 (2001): n. pag. *NARA*. Web. 16 Oct. 2015.

9. "African Americans in the Civil War: Equality Earned with Blood." *National Geographic*. National Geographic Society, 2008. Web. 16 Oct. 2015.

10. Kai Wright. *Soldiers of Freedom: An Illustrated History of African Americans in the Armed Forces*. New York: Black Dog & Leventhal, 2002. Print. 78.

11. Melvin Claxton and Mark Puls. *Uncommon Valor: A Story of Race, Patriotism, and Glory in the Final Battles of the Civil War*. Hoboken, NJ: Wiley, 2006. Print. 114.

12. Ibid. 116.

CHAPTER 8. SURRENDER AND RECONSTRUCTION

1. "Freedmen's Bureau." *History.com*. A&E Television Networks, 2010. Web. 10 Nov. 2015.

2. "Black Leaders During Reconstruction." *History.com*. A&E Television Networks, 2010. Web. 10 Nov. 2015.

3. Ibid.

INDEX

ABOUT THE AUTHOR

Kari Cornell is a freelance writer and editor who loves to read, garden, cook, run, and make clever things out of recycled materials. She is the author of *Women on the US Home Front*, *The Nitty Gritty Gardening Book: Fun Projects for All Seasons*, and countless biographies for kids. She lives in Minneapolis, Minnesota, with her husband, two sons, and a crazy dog named Emmylou.